Human Wishes

ALSO BY ROBERT HASS

POETRY

Sun Under Wood

Praise

Field Guide

TRANSLATIONS

Czeslaw Milosz, *The Separate Notebooks* (with Robert Pinsky and Renata Gorczynski)

Czeslaw Milosz, *Unattainable Earth* (with the author)

Czeslaw Milosz, *Collected Poems* (with the author and others)

Czeslaw Milosz, *Provinces* (with the author)

Czeslaw Milosz, *Facing the River* (with the author)

Czeslaw Milosz, *Road-side Dog* (with the author)

Czeslaw Milosz, *A Treatise on Poetry* (with the author)

The Essential Haiku: Versions of Bashō, Buson, and Issa

EDITOR

Robinson Jeffers, *Rock and Hawk: Shorter Poems*

Tomas Tranströmer, *Selected Poems: 1954–1986*

Into the Garden: A Wedding Anthology (with Stephen Mitchell)

Poet's Wishes:Poems for Everyday Life

American Poetry: The Twentieth Century (with John Hollander, Carolyn Kizer, Nathaniel Mackey, and Marjorie Perloff)

PROSE
Twentieth Century Pleasures: Prose on Poetry

ROBERT HASS

ecco

An Imprint of HarperCollins*Publishers*

Human Wishes

The author wishes to acknowledge the editors of the following magazines, in which some of these poems have appeared: *American Poetry Review, Antæus, Berkeley Poetry Review, East Bay Express, Ironwood, The New England Review, The New Republic, Verse, ZYZZYVA.* "January" first appeared in *19 New Poets of the Golden Gate,* edited by Philip Dow.

LIBRARY OF CONGRESS CATALOGING-IN-PUBLICATION DATA
Hass, Robert.
  Human Wishes.
  (The American poetry series)
  I. Title. II. Series: American poetry series
(Ecco Press)
PS3558.A725H84   1989   811'.54   88-16361

ISBN 0-88001-211-0 (cloth)
ISBN 0-88001-212-9 (paper)

Original publication of this book was made possible in part by a grant from the National Endowment for the Arts.
The text of this book is set in Bodoni Book.

08 09 10 **RRD** 20 19 18 17

Contents

1.

Spring Drawing

A man thinks *lilacs against white houses,* having seen them in the farm country south of Tacoma in April, and can't find his way to a sentence, a brushstroke carrying the energy of *brush* and *stroke*

—as if he were stranded on the aureole of the memory of a woman's breast,

and she, after the drive from the airport and a chat with her mother and a shower, which is ritual cleansing and a passage through water to mark transition,

had walked up the mountain on a summer evening.

Away from, not toward. As if the garden roses were a little hobby of the dead. As if the deer pellets in the pale grass and the wavering moon and the rondure—as they used to say, upping the ante—of heaven

were admirable completely, but only as common nouns of a plainer intention, *moon, shit, sky,*

as if spirit attended to plainness only, the more complicated forms exhausting it, tossed-off grapestems becoming crystal chandeliers,

as if radiance were the meaning of meaning, and justice responsible to daydream not only for the strict beauty of denial,

but as a felt need to reinvent the inner form of wishing.

Only the force of the brushstroke keeps the lilacs from pathos — the hes and shes of the comedy may or may not get together, but if they are to get at all,

then the interval created by *if,* to which mind and breath attend, nervous as the grazing animals the first brushes painted,

has become habitable space, lived in beyond wishing.

Vintage

They had agreed, walking into the delicatessen on Sixth Avenue, that their friends' affairs were focused and saddened by massive projection;

movie screens in their childhood were immense, and someone had proposed that need was unlovable.

The delicatessen had a chicken salad with chunks of cooked chicken in a creamy basil mayonnaise a shade lighter than the Coast Range in August; it was gray outside, February.

Eating with plastic forks, walking and talking in the sleety afternoon, they passed a house where Djuna Barnes was still, reportedly, making sentences.

Bashō said: avoid adjectives of scale, you will love the world more and desire it less.

And there were other propositions to consider: childhood, VistaVision, a pair of wet, mobile lips on the screen at least eight feet long.

On the corner a blind man with one leg was selling pencils. He must have received a disability check,

but it didn't feed his hunger for public agony, and he sat on the sidewalk slack-jawed, with a tin cup, his face and opaque eyes turned upward in a look of blind, questing pathos —

half Job, half mole.

Would the good Christ of Manhattan have restored his sight and two-thirds of his left leg? Or would he have healed his heart and left him there in a mutilated body? And what would that peace feel like?

It makes you want, at this point, a quick cut, or a reaction shot. "The taxis rivered up Sixth Avenue." "A little sunlight touched the steeple of the First Magyar Reform Church."

In fact, the clerk in the liquor store was appalled. "No, no," he said, "that cabernet can't be drunk for another five years."

Spring Rain

Now the rain is falling, freshly, in the intervals between sunlight,

a Pacific squall started no one knows where, drawn east as the drifts of warm air make a channel;

it moves its own way, like water or the mind,

and spills this rain passing over. The Sierras will catch it as last snow flurries before summer, observed only by the wakened marmots at ten thousand feet,

and we will come across it again as larkspur and penstemon sprouting along a creek above Sonora Pass next August,

where the snowmelt will have trickled into Dead Man's Creek and the creek spilled into the Stanislaus and the Stanislaus into the San Joaquin and the San Joaquin into the slow salt marshes of the bay.

That's not the end of it: the gray jays of the mountains eat larkspur seeds, which cannot propagate otherwise.

To simulate the process, you have to soak gathered seeds all night in the acids of coffee

and then score them gently with a very sharp knife before you plant them in the garden.

You might use what was left of the coffee we drank in Lisa's kitchen visiting.

There were orange poppies on the table in a clear glass vase, stained near the bottom to the color of sunrise;

the unstated theme was the blessedness of gathering and the blessing of dispersal—

it made you glad for beauty like that, casual and intense, lasting as long as the poppies last.

Late Spring

And then in mid-May the first morning of steady heat,

the morning, Leif says, when you wake up, put on shorts, and that's it for the day,

when you pour coffee and walk outside, blinking in the sun.

Strawberries have appeared in the markets, and peaches will soon;

squid is so cheap in the fishstores you begin to consult Japanese and Italian cookbooks for the various and ingenious ways of preparing *ika* and *calamari;*

and because the light will enlarge your days, your dreams at night will be as strange as the jars of octopus you saw once in a fisherman's boat under the summer moon;

and after swimming, white wine; and the sharing of stories before dinner is prolonged because the relations of the children in the neighborhood have acquired village intensity and the stories take longer telling;

and there are the nights when the fog rolls in that nobody likes—hey, fog, the Miwok sang, who lived here first, you better go home, pelican is beating your wife—

and after dark in the first cool hour, your children sleep so heavily in their beds exhausted from play, it is a pleasure to watch them,

Leif does not move a muscle as he lies there; no, wait; it is Luke who lies there in his eight-year-old body,

Leif is taller than you are and he isn't home; when he is, his feet will extend past the end of the mattress, and Kristin is at the corner in the dark, talking to neighborhood boys;

things change; there is no need for this dream-compelled narration; the rhythm will keep me awake, changing.

Rusia en 1931

The archbishop of San Salvador is dead, murdered by no one knows who. The left says the right, the right says provocateurs.

But the families in the barrios sleep with their children beside them and a pitchfork, or a rifle if they have one.

And posterity is grubbing in the footnotes to find out who the bishop is,

or waiting for the poet to get back to his business. Well, there's this:

her breasts are the color of brown stones in moonlight, and paler in moonlight.

And that should hold them for a while. The bishop is dead. Poetry proposes no solutions: it says justice is the well water of the city of Novgorod, black and sweet.

César Vallejo died on a Thursday. It might have been malaria, no one is sure; it burned through the small town of Santiago de Chuco in an Andean valley in his childhood; it may very well have flared in his veins in Paris on a rainy day;

and nine months later Osip Mandelstam was last seen feeding off the garbage heap of a transit camp near Vladivostok.

They might have met in Leningrad in 1931, on a corner; two men about forty; they could have compared gray hair at the temples, or compared reviews of *Trilce* and *Tristia* in 1922.

What French they would have spoken! And what the one thought would save Spain killed the other.

"I am no wolf by blood," Mandelstam wrote that year. "Only an equal could break me."

And Vallejo: "Think of the unemployed. Think of the forty million families of the hungry. . . ."

Spring Drawing 2

A man says *lilacs against white houses, two sparrows, one streaked, in a thinning birch*, and can't find his way to a sentence.

In order to be respectable, Thorstein Veblen said, desperate in Palo Alto, a thing must be wasteful, i.e., "a selective adaptation of forms to the end of conspicuous waste."

So we try to throw nothing away, as Keith, making dinner for us as his grandmother had done in Jamaica, left nothing; the kitchen was as clean at the end as when he started; even the shrimp shells and carrot fronds were part of the process,

and he said, when we tried to admire him, "Listen, I should send you into the chickenyard to look for a rusty nail to add to the soup for iron."

The first temptation of Sakyamuni was desire, but he saw that it led to fulfillment and then to desire, so that one was easy.

Because I have pruned it badly in successive years, the climbing rose has sent out, among the pale pink floribunda, a few wild white roses from the rootstalk.

Suppose, before they said *silver* or *moonlight* or *wet grass*, each poet had to agree to be responsible for the innocence of all the suffering on earth,

because they learned in arithmetic, during the long school days, that if there was anything left over, you had to carry it. The wild rose looks weightless, the floribunda are heavy with the richness and sadness of Europe

as they imitate the dying, petal by petal, of the people who bred them.

You hear pain singing in the nerves of things; it is not a song.

The gazelle's head turned; three jackals are eating his entrails and he is watching.

2.

Calm

1

September sun, a little fog in the mornings. No sanctified terror. At night Luke says, "How do you connect a *b* to an *a* in cursive?" He is bent to the task with such absorption that he doesn't notice the Scarlatti on the stereo, which he would in other circumstances turn off. He has said that chamber music sounds to him worried. I go out and look at the early stars. They glow faintly; faintly the mountain is washed in the color of sunset, at that season a faded scarlet like the petals of the bougainvillea which is also fading. A power saw, somewhere in the neighborhood, is enacting someone's idea of more pleasure, an extra room or a redwood tub. It hums and stops, hums and stops.

2

In the dream there was a face saying no. Not with words. Brow furrow, crow's-feet, lip curl: no, it is forbidden to you, no. But it was featureless, you could put your hand through it and feel cold on the other side. It was not the father-face saying no among the torsos and the pillars of aluminum nor the mother-face weeping no, no, no at the gate that guards rage; it was not even the idiot face of the obedient brother tacking his list of a hundred and seventy-five reasons why not on the greenhouse door. This face spits on archetypes, spits on caves, rainbows, the little human luxury of historical explanation. The meadow, you remember the meadow? And the air in June which held the scent of it as the woman in religious iconography holds the broken son? You can go into that meadow, the light routed by a brilliant tenderness of green, a cool V carved by a muskrat in the blue-gray distance of the pond, black-eyed Susans everywhere. You can go there.

Museum

On the morning of the Käthe Kollwitz exhibit, a young man and woman come into the museum restaurant. She is carrying a baby; he carries the air-freight edition of the Sunday *New York Times*. She sits in a high-backed wicker chair, cradling the infant in her arms. He fills a tray with fresh fruit, rolls, and coffee in white cups and brings it to the table. His hair is tousled, her eyes are puffy. They look like they were thrown down into sleep and then yanked out of it like divers coming up for air. He holds the baby. She drinks coffee, scans the front page, butters a roll and eats it in their little corner in the sun. After a while, she holds the baby. He reads the *Book Review* and eats some fruit. Then he holds the baby while she finds the section of the paper she wants and eats fruit and smokes. They've hardly exchanged a look. Meanwhile, I have fallen in love with this equitable arrangement, and with the baby who cooperates by sleeping. All around them are faces Käthe Kollwitz carved in wood of people with no talent or capacity for suffering who are suffering the numbest kinds of pain: hunger, helpless terror. But this young couple is reading the Sunday paper in the sun, the baby is sleeping, the green has begun to emerge from the rind of the cantaloupe, and everything seems possible.

Novella

A woman who, as a thirteen-year-old girl, develops a friendship with a blind painter, a painter who is going blind. She is Catholic, lives in the country. He rents a cabin from her father, and she walks through the woods — redwood, sword fern, sorrel — to visit him. He speaks to her as an equal and shows her his work. He has begun to sculpt but still paints, relying on color and the memory of line. He also keeps English biscuits in a tin and gives her one each visit. She would like more but he never gives her more. When he undresses her, she sometimes watches him, watches his hands which are thick and square, or his left eye with a small cloud like gray phlegm on the retina. But usually not. Usually she thinks of the path to his house, whether deer had eaten the tops of the fiddleheads, why they don't eat the peppermint saprophytes sprouting along the creek; or she visualizes the approach to the cabin, its large windows, the fuchsias in front of it where Anna's hummingbirds always hover with dirty green plumage and jeweled throats. Sometimes she thinks about her dream, the one in which her mother wakes up with no hands. The cabin smells of oil paint, but also of pine. The painter's touch is sexual and not sexual, as she herself is. From time to time she remembers this interval in the fall and winter of ninth grade. By spring the painter had moved. By summer her period had started. And after that her memory blurred, speeding up. One of her girlfriends frenchkissed a boy on a Friday night in the third row from the back at the Tamalpais theater. The other betrayed her and the universe by beginning to hang out with the popular girls whose fathers bought them cars. When the memory of that time came to her, it was touched by strangeness because it formed no pattern with the other events in her life. It lay in her memory like one piece of broken tile, salmon-colored or the deep green of wet leaves, beautiful in itself but unusable in the design she was making. Just the other day she remembered it. Her friends were coming up from the beach with a bucket full of something, smiling and waving to her, shouting something funny she couldn't make out, and suddenly she was there—the light flooding through the big windows, the litter of canvases, a white half-finished torso on the worktable, the sweet, wheaty odor of biscuits rising from the just-opened tin.

Churchyard

Somerset Maugham said a professional was someone who could do his best work when he didn't particularly feel like it. There was a picture of him in the paper, a face lined deeply and morally like Auden's, an old embittered tortoise, the corners of the mouth turned down resolutely to express the idea that everything in life is small change. And what he said when he died: I'm all through, the clever young men don't write essays about me. In the fleshly world, the red tulip in the garden sunlight is almost touched by shadow and begins to close up. Someone asked me yesterday: are deer monogamous? I thought of something I had read. When deer in the British Isles were forced to live in the open because of heavy foresting, it stunted them. The red deer who lived in the Scottish highlands a thousand years ago were a third larger than the present animal. This morning, walking into the village to pick up the car, I thought of a roof where I have slept in the summer in New York, pigeons in the early morning sailing up Fifth Avenue and silence in which you imagine the empty canyons the light hasn't reached yet. I was standing on the high street in Shelford, outside the fussy little teashop, and I thought a poem with the quick, lice-ridden pigeons in it might end: this is a dawn song in Manhattan. I hurried home to write it and, as I passed the churchyard, school was letting out. Luke was walking toward me smiling. He thought I had come to meet him. That was when I remembered the car, when he was walking toward me through the spring flowers and the eighteenth-century gravestones, his arms full of school drawings he hoped not to drop in the mud.

Conversion

Walking down the stairs this morning in the bitter cold, in the old house's salt smell of decay, past the Mansergh family coat of arms on the landing, I longed for California and thought I smelled laurel leaves: riding an acacia limb in the spring, rivers of yellow pollen, wild fennel we broke into six-inch lengths and threw at each other in the neighborhood wars or crouched in thickets of broom, shooting blue jays with BB guns. *Oiseaux*, I read last week when I picked up a volume of Ponge in the bookshop on rue Racine and thought of blue jays and so bought the Ponge, thinking I would write grave, luminous meditative poems. And walking across the bridge later past Notre Dame, I remembered Jack Kjellen who lived with his mother the telephone operator and who always wanted to pretend that we were the children of Fatima having a vision of the Virgin, and I would have to go along for a while, hoping to lure him back to playing pirates. Vision of Jack kneeling under the fig tree, palms prayerfully touching, looking up awed and reverent into the branches where the fat green figs hung like so many scrotums among the leaves. Scrota? But they were less differentiated than that: breasts, bottoms. The sexual ambiguity of flowers and fruits in French botanical drawings. Oh yes, sweet hermaphrodite peaches and the glister of plums!

Human Wishes

This morning the sun rose over the garden wall and a rare blue sky leaped from east to west. Man is altogether desire, say the Upanishads. Worth anything, a blue sky, says Mr. Acker, the Shelford gardener. Not altogether. In the end. Last night on television the ethnologist and the cameraman watched with hushed wonder while the chimpanzee carefully stripped a willow branch and inserted it into the anthill. He desired red ants. When they crawled slowly up the branch, he ate them, pinched between long fingers as the zoom lens enlarged his face. Sometimes he stopped to examine one, as if he were a judge at an ant beauty contest or God puzzled suddenly by the idea of suffering. There was an empty place in the universe where that branch wasn't and the chimp filled it, as Earlene, finding no back on an old Welsh cupboard she had bought in Saffron Walden, imagined one there and imagined both the cupboard and the imagined back against a kitchen wall in Berkeley, and went into town looking for a few boards of eighteenth-century tongue-in-groove pine to fill that empty space. I stayed home to write, or rather stayed home and stared at a blank piece of paper, waiting for her to come back, thinking tongue-in-groove, tongue-in-groove, as if language were a kind of moral cloud chamber through which the world passed and from which it emerged charged with desire. The man in the shop in Cambridge said he didn't have any old pine, but when Earlene went back after thinking about it to say she was sure she had seen some, the man found it. Right under his feet, which was puzzling. Mr. Acker, hearing the story, explained. You know, he said, a lot of fiddling goes on in those places. The first time you went in, the governor was there, the second time he wasn't, so the chap sold you some scrap and he's four quid in pocket. No doubt he's having a good time now with his mates in the pub. Or he might have put it on the horses at Newmarket. He might parley it into a fortune.

Tall Windows

All day you didn't cry or cry out and you felt like sleeping. The desire to sleep was light bulbs dimming as a powerful appliance kicks on. You recognized that. As in school it was explained to you that pus was a brave army of white corpuscles hurling themselves at the virulent invader and dying. Riding through the Netherlands on a train, you noticed that even the junk was neatly stacked in the junkyards. There were magpies in the fields beside the watery canals, neat little houses, tall windows. In Leiden, on the street outside the university, the house where Descartes lived was mirrored in the canal. There was a pair of swans and a sense that, without haste or anxiety, all the people on the street were going to arrive at their appointments punctually. Swans and mirrors. And Descartes. It was easy to see how this European tranquillity would produce a poet like Mallarmé, a middle-class art like symbolism. And you did not despise the collective orderliness, the way the clerks in the stores were careful to put bills in the cash register with the Queen's face facing upward. In the house next to the house where Descartes lived, a Jewish professor died in 1937. His wife was a Dutch woman of strict Calvinist principles and she was left with two sons. When the Nazis came in 1940, she went to court and perjured herself by testifying that her children were conceived during an illicit affair with a Gentile, and when she developed tuberculosis in 1943, she traded passports with a Jewish friend, since she was going to die anyway, and took her place on the train to the camps. Her sons kissed her good-bye on the platform. Eyes open. What kept you awake was a feeling that everything in the world has its own size, that if you found its size among the swellings and diminishings it would be calm and shine.

The Harbor at Seattle

They used to meet one night a week at a place on top of Telegraph Hill to explicate Pound's *Cantos* — Peter who was a scholar; and Linda who could recite many of the parts of the poem that envisioned paradise; and Bob who wanted to understand the energy and surprise of its music; and Bill who knew Greek and could tell them that "Dioce, whose terraces were the color of stars," was a city in Asia Minor mentioned by Herodotus.

And that winter when Bill locked his front door and shot himself in the heart with one barrel of a twelve-gauge Browning over-and-under, the others remembered the summer nights, after a long session of work, when they would climb down the steep stairs that negotiated the cliff where the hill faced the waterfront to go somewhere to get a drink and talk. The city was all lights at that hour and the air smelled of coffee and the bay.

In San Francisco coffee is a family business, and a profitable one, so that members of the families are often on the society page of the newspaper, which is why Linda remembered the wife of one of the great coffee merchants, who had also killed herself; it was a memory from childhood, from those first glimpses a newspaper gives of the shape of the adult world, and it mixed now with the memory of the odor of coffee and the salt air.

And Peter recalled that the museum had a photograph of that woman by Minor White. They had all seen it. She had bobbed hair and a smart suit on with sharp lapels and padded shoulders, and her skin was perfectly clear. Looking directly into the camera, she does not seem happy but she seems confident; and it is as if Minor White understood that her elegance, because it was a matter of style, was historical, because behind her is an old barn which is the real subject of the picture—the grain of its wood planking so sharply focused that it seems alive, grays and blacks in a rivery and complex pattern of venation.

The back of Telegraph Hill was not always so steep. At the time of the earthquake, building materials were scarce, so coastal ships made a good thing of hauling lumber down from the northwest. But the economy was paralyzed, there were no goods to take back north, so they dynamited the side of the hill and used the blasted rock for ballast, and then, in port again, they dumped the rock in the water to take on more lumber, and that was how they built the harbor in Seattle.

Paschal Lamb

Well, David had said—it was snowing outside and his voice contained
many registers of anger, disgust, and wounded justice, I think it's crazy.
I'm not going to be a sacrificial lamb.

In Greece sometimes, a friend told me, when she walked on the high
road above the sea back to her house from the village in the dark, and the
sky seemed immense, the moon terribly bright, she wondered if her life
would be a fit gift.

And there is that poor heifer in the poem by Keats, all decked out in
ribbons and flowers, no terror in the eyes, no uncontrollable slobber of
mucus at the muzzle, since she didn't understand the festivities.

And years later, after David had quit academic life, he actually bought a
ranch in Kentucky near a town called Pleasureville, and began to raise
sheep.

When we visited that summer and the nights were shrill with crickets
and the heat did not let up, we traded stories after dinner and he told us
again the story about his first teaching job and the vice-president.

When he bought the place, he had continued his subscriptions to *The
Guardian* and *Workers' Vanguard*, but they piled up in a corner unread.
He had a mortgage to pay. He didn't know a thing about raising animals
for slaughter, and so he read *The American Sheepman* with an intensity
of concentration he had never even approximated when he was reading
political theory for his Ph.D. orals.

The vice-president of the United States, after his term in office, accepted a position as lecturer in political science at a small college in his home district, where David had just taken his first job. The dean brought Hubert Humphrey around to introduce him to the faculty. When they came to David's office, the vice-president, expensively dressed, immensely hearty, extended his hand and David did not feel he could take it because he believed the man was a war criminal; and not knowing any way to avoid the awkwardness, he said so, which was the beginning of his losing the job at that college.

But that was the dean's doing. The vice-president started to cry. He had the hurt look, David said, of a kicked dog with a long, unblemished record of loyalty and affection, this man who had publicly defended, had *praised* the terror bombing of villages full of peasants. He seemed to David unimaginably empty of inner life if he could be hurt rather than affronted by a callow young man making a stiffly moral gesture in front of two men his father's age. David said that he had never looked at another human being with such icy, wondering detachment, and that he hadn't liked the sensation.

And so in the high-ceilinged kitchen, in the cricket-riddled air drenched with the odor of clover, we remembered Vic Doyno in the snow in Buffalo, in the days when the war went on continuously like a nightmare in our waking and sleeping hours.

Vic had come to work flushed with excitement at an idea he had had in the middle of the night. He had figured out how to end the war. It was a simple plan. Everyone in the country — in the world, certainly a lot of

Swedish and English students would go along—who was opposed to the war would simply cut off the little finger on the left hand and send it to the president. Imagine! They would arrive slowly at first, the act of one or two maniacs, but the news would hit the newspapers and the next day there would be a few more. And the day after that more. And on the fourth day there would be thousands. And on the fifth day, clinics would be set up—organized by medical students in Madison, San Francisco, Stockholm, Paris—to deal with the surgical procedure safely and on a massive scale. And on the sixth day, the war would stop. It would stop. The helicopters at Bienhoa would sit on the airfields in silence like squads of disciplined mosquitoes. Peasants, worried and curious because peasants are always worried and curious, would stare up curiously into the unfamiliar quiet of a blue, cirrus-drifted sky. And years later we would know each other by those missing fingers. An aging Japanese businessman minus a little finger on his left hand would notice the similarly mutilated hand of his cab driver in Chicago, and they would exchange a fleeting unspoken nod of fellowship.

And it could happen. All we had to do to make it happen—Vic had said, while the water for tea hissed on the hot plate in David's chilly office and the snow came down thick as cotton batting, was cut off our little fingers right now, take them down to the department secretary, and have her put them in the mail.

Duck Blind

He was a judge in Louisiana—this is a story told by his daughter over dinner—and duck hunting was the one passion in his life. Every year during the season when the birds migrate, green-headed mallards and pintails and canvasbacks, blue-winged teal and cinnamon teal, gadwall and widgeon and scaup carried by some inward reckoning down wide migration routes in orderly flocks from Canada to Yucatán, he rose at three in the morning and hunted them. Now, at seventy-five, he still goes every day to the blind; he belongs to a club with other white men who, every morning, fathers and sons, draw lots before sunup and row quietly in skiffs to their positions. When he misses a shot, he shakes his head and says, "To shoot a duck"—it is what hunters often say—"you have to be a duck." And many mornings now he falls asleep. When five sprig circle, making a perfect pass above his blind, and all the men hold their breath and hear the silky sound of wind in the oiled feathers of the birds, and nothing happens, only silence, one of his companions will whisper to his son, "Goddammit, I think the judge is asleep again." And if it happens twice, he says, "Lennie, you better row over there and see if the judge is asleep or dead." And the son, a middle-aged man, balding, with thick, inarticulate hands, rows toward the judge's blind in the ground mist, and watches the birds veer off into the first light of the south sky.

Quartet

The two couples having dinner on Saturday night — it is late fall — are in their late thirties and stylish, but not slavishly so. The main course is French, loin of pork probably, with a North African accent, and very good. The dessert will be sweet and fresh, having to do with cream and berries (it is early fall), and it feels like a course, it is that substantial. They are interestingly employed: a professor of French, let's say, the assistant curator of film at a museum, a research director for a labor union, a psychologist (a journalist, a sculptor, an astronomer, etc.). One of them believes that after death there is nothing, that our knowledge of this is a fluke, or a joke like knocking on doors as children sometimes do, and then disappearing so that the pleasure has to be in imagining the dismay of the person who finds the entryway empty. Another believes dimly and from time to time not in heaven exactly, but in a place where the dead can meet and talk quietly, where losses are made good. Another believes in the transmigration of souls, not the cosmic reform school of Indian religion, but an unplanned passage rather like life in its mixture of randomness and affinity. The fourth believes in ghosts, or has felt that consciousness might take longer to perish than the body and linger sometimes as spectral and unfinished grief, or unfinished happiness, if it doesn't come to the same thing. They are not talking about this. They are talking about high school (children, travel, politics — they know more or less who is paying for their meal). Four people, the women with soft breasts, the men with soft, ropy external genitals. In chairs, talking. It is probably the third Saturday in September. Maybe they have had melon or a poached pear. The hostess, a solid, placid woman with unusually large knuckles and a good amateur soprano voice, has begun to pour coffee into cream-colored cups.

A Story About the Body

The young composer, working that summer at an artist's colony, had watched her for a week. She was Japanese, a painter, almost sixty, and he thought he was in love with her. He loved her work, and her work was like the way she moved her body, used her hands, looked at him directly when she made amused and considered answers to his questions. One night, walking back from a concert, they came to her door and she turned to him and said, "I think you would like to have me. I would like that too, but I must tell you that I have had a double mastectomy," and when he didn't understand, "I've lost both my breasts." The radiance that he had carried around in his belly and chest cavity — like music — withered very quickly, and he made himself look at her when he said, "I'm sorry. I don't think I could." He walked back to his own cabin through the pines, and in the morning he found a small blue bowl on the porch outside his door. It looked to be full of rose petals, but he found when he picked it up that the rose petals were on top; the rest of the bowl — she must have swept them from the corners of her studio — was full of dead bees.

In the Bahamas

The doctor looked at her stitches thoughtfully. A tall lean white man with an English manner. "Have you ever watched your mum sew?" he asked. "The fellow who did this hadn't. I like to take a tuck on the last stitch. That way the skin doesn't bunch up on the ends. Of course, you can't see the difference, but you can feel it." Later she asked him about all the one-armed and one-legged black men she kept seeing in the street. "Diabetic gangrene, mostly. There really isn't more of it here than in your country, but there's less prosthesis. It's expensive, of course. And stumps are rather less of a shock when you come right down to it. Well, as we say, there's nothing colorful about the Caribbean." He tapped each black thread into a silver basin as he plucked it out. "Have you ever been to Haiti? Now there is a truly appalling place."

January

> Three clear days
> and then a sudden storm —
> the waxwings, having
> feasted on the pyracantha,
> perch in the yard
> on an upended pine, and face
> into the slanting rain.
> I think they are a little drunk.

I was making this gathering — which pleased me, the waxwings that always pass through at this time of year, the discarded Christmas tree they perched in, and the first January storm, as if I had finally defined a California season — when Rachel came down the walk and went into the house. I typed out the poem — the birds giddy with Janus, the two-faced god — and then went in to say hello.

> Two women sitting at a kitchen table
> Muted light on a rainy morning
> One has car keys in her hand

I was surprised by two feelings at once; one was a memory, the other a memory-trace. The memory, called up, I think, by a glimpse of Rachel's sculpted profile against the cypresses outside the kitchen window just before she turned to greet me: I thought of a day twelve years ago in early summer. Rachel had just had an abortion and we all went for a walk in San Francisco near the bay. Everything was in bloom and we were being conscientiously cheerful, young really, not knowing what form there might be for such an occasion or, in fact, what occasion it was. And

Rachel, in profile, talking casually, the bay behind her, looked radiant with grief. The memory-trace had to do with car keys and two women in a kitchen. Someone was visiting my mother. It was a rainy day so I was inside. Her friend, as adults will, to signal that they are not going to take too much of your time, had car keys in her hand. Between Earlene and Rachel, there were three oranges in a basket on a table and I had the sweet, dizzying sensation that the color was circulating among them in a dance.

> Sing the hymeneal slow.
> Lovers have a way to go,
> Their lightest bones will have to grow
> More heavy in uneasy heat.
> The heart is what we eat
> With almond blossoms bitter to the tongue,
> The hair of tulips
> In the softening spring.

Rachel is looking for a house. A realtor had just shown her one. Looking at the new house, she loved the old one, especially the green of the garden, looking out on the garden. The old house has drawbacks, long rehearsed, and the new one, with its cedar shingle, exposed beams, view, doesn't feel right, it is so anonymous and perfect; it doesn't have the green secrecy of the garden or the apple tree to tie Lucia's swing to. Earlene is asking questions, trying to help. A few minutes later, when I pass through again, they are laughing. At the comedy in the business of trying to sort through mutually exclusive alternatives in which figures some tacit imagination of contentment, some invisible symbolizing need from which life wants to flower. "I hate that old house," Rachel is saying, laughing, tears in her eyes. But that is not mainly what I notice; I find myself looking at the women's skin, the coloring, and the first relaxation of the tautness of the sleeker skin of the young, the casual beauty and formality of that first softening.

> Back at my desk: no birds, no rain,
> but light—the white of Shasta daisies,
> and two red geraniums against the fence,
> and the dark brown of wet wood,
> glistening a little as it dries.

3.

The Apple Trees at Olema

They are walking in the woods along the coast
and in a grassy meadow, wasting, they come upon
two old neglected apple trees. Moss thickened
every bough and the wood of the limbs looked rotten
but the trees were wild with blossom and a green fire
of small new leaves flickered even on the deadest branches.
Blue-eyes, crane's-bills, little Dutchmen
flecked the meadow, and an intricate, leopard-spotted
leaf-green flower whose name they didn't know.
Trout lily, he said; she said, adder's-tongue.
She is shaken by the raw, white, backlit flaring
of the apple blossoms. He is exultant,
as if some thing he felt were verified,
and looks to her to mirror his response.
If it is afternoon, a thin moon of my own dismay
fades like a scar in the sky to the east of them.
He could be knocking wildly at a closed door
in a dream. She thinks, meanwhile, that moss
resembles seaweed drying lightly on a dock.
Torn flesh, it was the repetitive torn flesh
of appetite in the cold white blossoms
that had startled her. Now they seem tender
and where she was repelled she takes the measure
of the trees and lets them in. But he no longer
has the apple trees. This is as sad or happy
as the tide, going out or coming in, at sunset.
The light catching in the spray that spumes up
on the reef is the color of the lesser finch

they notice now flashing dull gold in the light
above the field. They admire the bird together,
it draws them closer, and they start to walk again.
A small boy wanders corridors of a hotel that way.
Behind one door, a maid. Behind another one, a man
in striped pajamas shaving. He holds the number
of his room close to the center of his mind
gravely and delicately, as if it were the key,
and then he wanders among strangers all he wants.

Misery and Splendor

Summoned by conscious recollection, she
would be smiling, they might be in a kitchen talking,
before or after dinner. But they are in this other room,
the window has many small panes, and they are on a couch
embracing. He holds her as tightly
as he can, she buries herself in his body.
Morning, maybe it is evening, light
is flowing through the room. Outside,
the day is slowly succeeded by night,
succeeded by day. The process wobbles wildly
and accelerates: weeks, months, years. The light in the room
does not change, so it is plain what is happening.
They are trying to become one creature,
and something will not have it. They are tender
with each other, afraid
their brief, sharp cries will reconcile them to the moment
when they fall away again. So they rub against each other,
their mouths dry, then wet, then dry.
They feel themselves at the center of a powerful
and baffled will. They feel
they are an almost animal,
washed up on the shore of a world—
or huddled against the gate of a garden—
to which they can't admit they can never be admitted.

Santa Lucia II

Pleasure is so hard to remember. It goes
so quick from the mind. That day in third grade,
I thought I heard the teacher say the ones
who finished the assignment could go home.
I had a new yellow rubber raincoat
with a hat, blue galoshes; I put them on,
took my lunchpail and my books and started
for the door. The whole class giggled. Somehow
I had misheard. "Where are *you* going?"
the teacher said. The kids all roared. I froze.
In yellow rubber like a bathtub toy.
That memory comes when I call, vivid,
large and embarrassing like the helpless
doglike fidelity of my affections,
and I flush each time. But the famous night
we first made love, I think I remember
stars, that the moon was watery and pale.

It always circles back to being seen.
Psyche in the dark, Psyche in the daylight
counting seed. We go to the place where words
aren't and we die, suffer resurrection
two by two. Some men sleep, some read, some
want chocolate in the middle of the night.
They look at you adoring and you wonder
what it is they think they see. Themselves
transformed, adored. Oh, it makes me tired
and it doesn't work. On the floor in the sunlight

he looked sweet. Laughing, hair tangled, he said
I was all he wanted. If he were all I
wanted, he'd be life. I saw from the window
Mrs. Piombo in the backyard, planting phlox
in her immaculate parable of a garden.
She wears her black sweater under the cypress
in the sun. Life fits her like a glove,
she doesn't seem to think it's very much.

Near Big Sur lighthouse, morning, dunes
of white sand the eelgrass holds in place.
I saw at a distance what looked like feet
lifted in the air. I was on the reef,
I thought I was alone in all the silence,
poking anemones, watching turban snails
slide across the brown kelp in tidal pools.
And then I saw them. It was all I saw—
a pair of ankles; lifted, tentative.
They twitched like eyelids, like a nerve jumping
in the soft flesh of the arm. My crotch throbbed
and my throat went dry. Absurd. Pico Blanco
in the distance and the summer heat steady
as a hand. I wanted to be touched
and didn't want to want it. And by whom?
The sea foamed easily around the rocks
like the pathos of every summer. In the pools

anemones, cream-colored, little womb-mouths,
oldest animal with its one job to do
I carry as a mystery inside
or else it carries me around it, petals
to its stamen. And then I heard her cry.
Sharp, brief, a gull's hunger bleeding off the wind.
A sound like anguish. Driving up the coast—
succulents ablaze on the embankments,
morning glory on the freeway roadcuts
where the rifles crackled at the army base—
I thought that life was hunger moving and
that hunger was a form of suffering.
The drive from the country to the city
was the distance from solitude to wanting,
or to union, or to something else—the city
with its hills and ill-lit streets, a vast
dull throb of light, dimming the night sky.

What a funny place to center longing,
in a stranger. All I have to do is reach
down once and touch his cheek and the long fall
from paradise begins. The dream in which
I'm stuck and father comes to help but then
takes off his mask, the one in which shit, oozing
from a wound, forms delicate rosettes, the dream
in which my book is finished and my shoulders
start to sprout a pelt of hair, or the woman

in the sari, prone, covered with menstrual
blood, her arms raised in supplication.
We take that into the dark. Sex is peace
because it's so specific. And metaphors:
live milk, blond hills, blood singing,
hilarity that comes and goes like rain,
you got me coffee, I'll get you your book,
something to sleep beside, with, against.

The morning light comes up, and their voices
through the wall, the matter-of-fact chatter
of the child dawdling at breakfast, a clink
of spoons. It's in small tasks the mirrors
disappear, the old woman already
gone shopping. Her apricot, pruned yesterday,
is bare. To be used up like that. Psyche
punished for her candle in the dark.
Oil painting is a form of ownership.
The essay writer who was here last year,
at someone's party, a heavy man with glasses,
Persian cat. Art since the Renaissance
is ownership. I should get down to work.
You and the task—the third that makes a circle
is the imagined end. You notice rhythms
washing over you, opening and closing,
they are the world, inside you, and you work.

Cuttings

Body Through Which the Dream Flows

You count up everything you have
or have let go.
What's left is the lost and the possible.
To the lost, the irretrievable
or just out of reach, you say:
light loved the pier, the seedy
string quartet of the sun going down over water
that gilds ants and beach fleas
ecstatic and communal on the stiffened body
of a dead grebe washed ashore
by last night's storm. Idiot sorrow,
an irregular splendor, is the half-sister
of these considerations.
To the possible you say nothing.
October on the planet.
Huge moon, bright stars.

The Lovers Undressing

They put on rising, and they rose.
They put on falling, and they fell.
They were the long grass on the hillside
that shudders in the wind. They sleep.
Days, kitchens. Cut flowers,
shed petals, smell of lemon, smell of toast

or soap. Are you upset about something,
one says. No, the other says.
Are you sure, the one says.
Yes, the other says, I'm sure.

Sad

Often we are sad animals.
Bored dogs, monkeys getting rained on.

Migration

A small brown wren in the tangle
of the climbing rose. April:
last rain, the first dazzle
and reluctance of the light.

Dark

Desire lies down with the day
and the night birds wake
to their fast heartbeats
in the trees. The woman beside you
is breathing evenly. All day
you were in a body. Now

you are in a skull. Wind,
streetlights, trees flicker
on the ceiling in the dark.

Things Change

Small song,
two beat:
the robin on the lawn
hops from sun
into shadow, shadow
into sun.

Stories in Bed

In the field behind her house, she said,
fennel grew high and green
in early summer, and the air
smelled like little anise-scented loaves
in the Italian restaurants her father
used to take them to on Sunday nights.
She had to sit up straight:
it was the idea of family
they failed at. She lights a cigarette,
remembering the taut veins
in her mother's neck, how she had studied them,

repelled. He has begun to drowse:
backyards, her voice, dusty fennel,
the festering sweetness of the plums.

Monday Morning, Late Summer

On the fence
in the sunlight,
beach towels.

No wind.

The apricots have ripened
and been picked.
The blackberries have ripened
and been picked.

So

They walked along the dry gully.
Cottonwoods, so the river must be underground.

Plus Which

She turned to him. Or, alternatively,
she turned away. Doves let loose
above the sea, or the sea at night
beating on the pylons of a bridge.
Off-season: the candles were mediterranean,
opaque, and the cat cried *olor,*
olor, olor in the blue susurrations
of heather by the outhouse door.

Santa Barbara Road

Mornings on the south side of the house
just outside the kitchen door
arrived early in summer—
when Luke was four or five
he would go out there, still in his dandelion-
yellow pajamas on May mornings
and lie down on the first warm stone.

For years, when the green nubs of apricots
first sprouted on the backyard tree,
I thought about a bench in that spot,
a redwood screen behind green brushstrokes
of bamboo, and one April, walking into the kitchen,
I felt like a stranger to my life
and it scared me, so when the gray doves returned
to the telephone wires
and the lemons were yellowing
and no other task presented itself,
I finally went into the garden and started
digging, trying to marry myself
and my hands to that place.

• • •

Household verses: "Who are you?"
the rubber duck in my hand asked Kristin
once, while she was bathing, three years old.
"Kristin," she said, laughing, her delicious
name, delicious self. "That's just your name,"

the duck said. "Who are you?" "Kristin,"
she said. "Kristin's a name. Who are you?"
the duck asked. She said, shrugging,
"Mommy, Daddy, Leif."

   ■   ■   ■

The valley behind the hills heats up,
vultures, red-tailed hawks floating in the bubbles
of warm air that pull the fog right in
from the ocean. You have to rise at sunup
to see it steaming through the Gate
in ghostly June. Later, on street corners,
you can hardly see the children, chirping
and shivering, each shrill voice climbing over
the next in an ascending chorus. "Wait, you guys,"
one little girl says, trying to be heard.
"Wait, wait, wait, wait, wait."
Bright clothes: the last buses of the term.

   ■   ■   ■

Richard arrives to read poems, the final guest
of a long spring. I thought of Little Shelford,
where we had seen him last. In the worked gold
of an English October, Kristin watched the neighbor's
horses wading in the meadowgrass, while Leif
and I spiraled a football by the chalk-green,
moss-mortared ruin of the garden wall.
Mr. Acker, who had worked in the village

since he was a boy, touched his tweed cap
mournfully. "Reminds me of the war," he said.
"Lots of Yanks here then." Richard rolled a ball
to Luke, who had an old alphabet book
in which cherubic animals disported.
Richard was a *rabbit* with a *roller.*
Luke evidently thought that it was droll
or magical that Richard, commanded
by the power of the word, was crouching
under the horse-chestnut, dangling
a hand-rolled cigarette and rolling him a ball.
He gave me secret, signifying winks, though
he could not quite close one eye at a time.
So many prisms to construct a moment!
Spiderwebs set at all angles on a hedge:
what Luke thought was going on, what Mr. Acker
saw, and Richard, who had recently divorced,
idly rolling a ball with someone else's child,
healing slowly, as the neighbor's silky mare
who had had a hard birth in the early spring,
stood quiet in the field as May grew sweet,
her torn vagina healing. So many visions
intersecting at what we call the crystal
of a common world, all the growing and shearing,
all the violent breaks. On Richard's last night
in Berkeley, we drank late and drove home
through the city gardens in the hills. Light
glimmered on the bay. Night-blooming jasmine

gave a heavy fragrance to the air. Richard
studied the moonlit azaleas in silence.
I knew he had a flat in East London.
I wondered if he was envying my life.
"How did you ever get stuck in this nest
of gentlefolk?" he said. "Christ! It's lovely.
I shouldn't want to live in America.
I'd miss the despair of European men."

. . .

Luke comes running in the house excited
to say that an Iceland poppy has "bloomed up."
His parents, who are not getting along
especially well, exchange wry looks.
They had both forgotten, since small children
were supposed to love flowers, that they actually
do. And there is the pathos of the metaphor
or myth: irresistible flowering.

. . .

Everything rises from the dead in June.
There is some treasure hidden in the heart of summer
everyone remembers now, and they can't be sure
the lives they live in will discover it.
They remember the smells of childhood vacations.
The men buy maps, raffish hats. Some women
pray to it by wearing blouses
with small buttons you have to button patiently,

as if to say, this is not winter, not
the cold shudder of dressing in the dark.

．　．　．

Howard, one child on his shoulder,
another trotting beside him, small hand
in his hand, is going to write a book—
"Miranda, stop pulling Daddy's hair"—about
the invention of the family in medieval France.
The ritual hikes of Memorial Day: adults
chatting in constantly re-forming groups,
men with men, women with women, couples,
children cozened along with orange sections
and with raisins, running ahead, and back,
and interrupting. Long views through mist
of the scaly brightness of the ocean,
the massive palisade of Point Reyes cliffs.
"I would have thought," a woman friend says,
peeling a tangerine for Howard whose hands
are otherwise employed, cautioning a child
to spit out all the seeds, "that biology
invented the family." A sudden upward turn
of the trail, islands just on the horizon,
blue. "Well," he says, "I think it's useful
to see it as a set of conventions."

．　．　．

Someone's great-aunt dies. Someone's sister's
getting married in a week. The details are comic.
But we dress, play flutes, twine flowers,
and read long swatches from the Song of Songs
to celebrate some subtle alteration
in a cohabitation that has, probably, reached a crisis
and solved it with the old idea of these vows.
To vow, and tear down time: one of the lovers gives up
an apartment, returned to and stripped piecemeal
over months or years, until one maidenhair fern
left by the kitchen window as a symbol, dwindling,
of the resilience of a solitary life
required watering. Now it too is moved.

• • •

Summer solstice: parents, if their children
are young enough, put them to bed before dark,
then sit to watch the sun set on the bay.
A woman brings her coffee to the view.
Dinner done. What was she thinking
before her mother called, before the neighbor
called about the car pool? Something,
something interesting. The fog flares
and smolders, salmon first, then rose,
and in the twilight the sound comes up
across the neighborhood backyards of a table
being set. Other lives with other schedules.
Then dark, and, veering eerily, a bat.

●　●　■

Body half-emerged from the bright blue cocoon
of the sleeping bag, he wakes, curled hand
curling toward the waves of his sister's
cut-short, slept-on and matted, cornfield-
colored hair. She stirs a little in her sleep.
Her mother, whose curved brow her brow exactly
echoes, stirs. What if the gnostics had it backward?
What if eternity is pure destruction? The child,
rubbing his eyes, stares drowsily at the sea,
squints at his father who is sitting up,
shivers from his bag, plods up the beach
to pee against the cliff, runs back, climbs in
with his mother, wriggles close. In a minute
he'll be up again, fetching driftwood for a fire.

■　●　■

Leif comes home from the last day of his sophomore year.
I am sitting on the stoop by our half-dug,
still-imagined kitchen porch, reading
Han Dynasty rhyme-prose. He puts a hand on my shoulder,
grown to exactly my height and still growing.
"Dad," he says, "I'm not taking any more
of this tyrannical bullshit." I read to him
from Chia Ya: *The great man is without bent,*
a million changes are as one to him.
He says: "And another thing, don't lay
your Buddhist trips on me." *The span of life is fated;*

man cannot guess its ending.
In stillness like the stillness of deep springs . . .
In the kitchen he flips the lid
of the blueberry yogurt. I am thinking
this project is more work than I want.
Joining, scattering, ebbing and flowing,
where is there persistence, where is there rule?
"Bullshit," he mutters, "what is the existential reality"—
he has just read *Nausea* in advanced English—
"of all this bullshit, Todo?"
Todo is the dog. It occurs to me
that I am not a very satisfying parent
to rebel against. *Like an unmoored boat*
drifting aimlessly, not even valuing
the breath of life, the wise man
embraces nothing, and drifts with it.

I look at his long body in a chair
and wonder if I'd tell him to embrace the void.
I think he will embrace a lover soon.
I want the stars to terrify him once. I want him
to weep bitterly when his grandfather dies,
hating the floral carpet, hating it that his old aunts
have become expert at an obscene event.
I would ward off, if I could, the thicket
of grief on grief in which Chia Ya
came to entire relinquishment as to a clearing.
Digging again, I say, "You know, I started this job

/ *58*

and I hate it already, and now I have to finish."
He leans against the doorpost with a spoon.
Takes a mouthful. "Well, Pop," he says, "that's life."

   • • •

Children stroll down to the lakeside
on a path already hot from the morning sun
and known well by them in its three turnings—
one by the sugar pine gouged with rusty nails
where summers past they put a hammock or a swing,
one by the thimbleberry where the walk seems driest,
dust heaviest on the broad soft leaves, and bees—
you have to be careful—are nuzzling in the flowers,
one by the aspens where the smell of water
starts and the path opens onto sand, the wide blue lake,
mountains on the farther shore. The smaller boy
has line, a can for crawfish, and an inner tube.
He's nursing a summer cold. His older brother's
carrying a book, a towel, a paper on *Medea*
his girlfriend has mailed to him from summer school.
The girl has several books, some magazines.
She loves her family, but she's bored. She'd rather
be in town where her friends are, where her real life
has begun. They settle on the beach.
Cold water, hot sun, the whole of an afternoon.

Berkeley Eclogue

1.

Sunlight on the streets in afternoon
and shadows on the faces in the open-air cafés.
What for? Wrong question. You knock
without knowing that you knocked. The door
opens on a century of clouds and centuries
of centuries of clouds. The bird sings
among the toyons in the spring's diligence
of rain. *And then what? Hand on your heart.*
Would you die for spring? What would you die for?
Anything?
                    Anything. It may be I can't find it
and they can, the spooners of whipped cream
and espresso at the sunny tables, the women
with their children in the stores. *You want to sing?*
Tra-la. Empty and he wants to sing.
A pretty river, but there were no fish.
Smart fish. They will be feeding for a while.
He wants to sing. Yes, poverty or death.
Piety or death, you meant, you dope. You fool,
"bloody little fool." She slammed the door.
He was, of course, forlorn. And lorn and afterlorn.
It made a busy afternoon. The nights were difficult.
No doors, no drama. The moon ached aimlessly.
Dogs in the morning had their dog masks on.
It did not seem good, the moths, the apples?
The gold meander in her long brown hair
cast one vote then, sinuous as wrists. He attended
to her earnestness as well—and the child liked breakfast.

He believed in that. Every day was a present
he pretended that he brought. The sun came up.
Nothing to it. I'll do it again tomorrow,
and it did. Sundays he fetched croissants,
the frank nipples of brioche that say it's day,
eat up, the phone will ring, the mail arrive.
Someone who heard you sing the moths, the apples,
and they were—for sure they were, and good
though over there. Gold hair. A lucky guy
with a head on his shoulders, and all heart.
You can skip this part. The moths, the apples,
and the morning news. Apartheid, terror,
boys in a jungle swagging guns. *Injustice
in tropical climates is appalling,
and it does do you credit to think so.*
I knew that I had my own work to do.
The ones who wear the boots decide all that.
He wants to sing one thing so true that it is true.
I cast a vote across the river, skipped another
on the pond. It skittered for a while triumphantly,
then sank. And we were naked on the riverbank.
I believed a little in her breasts, the color
of the aureoles that afternoon, and something
she said about her sister that seemed shrewd.
Afterward we watched a woman making masks,
mostly with feathers and a plaster cast of face
she glued them to. The mouths formed cries.
They were the parts that weren't there—implied

by what surrounded them. They were a cunning
emptiness. *I think you ought to start again.*
The fish were smart. They mouthed the salmon eggs,
or so you felt. The boys kept reeling in.
Casting and reeling in. You'll never catch a fish
that way, you said. One caught a fish that way.
One perched in a chair abandoned on the sand.
Drank orange soda, watched his rod twitter
in a fork of willow twig. "I'm getting a bite, Dad."
It was the river current or the wind. In every
language in the world, I bet. *Do you believe
in that?* Not especially. It means the race is old.
And full of hope? *He wants to sing.*
You bastard, she said, and slammed the door.
You've been in this part already. Say "before."
"Before." She shut the door. It couldn't have been
otherwise. How sick you were. The mouths, the apples,
the buttons on a blouse. The bone was like pearl,
and small, and very shiny. The fat child's face
was flecked with Santa Rosa plum. She cried.
Her mother hit her. Then it seemed like blood.
A flood of tears, then. You remembered
never to interfere. It humiliates them.
They beat the child again when they get home.
It's only your feeling you assuage.
You didn't interfere. Her gold wandering of hair,
she told you that another time. The father
at the county fair was wailing on the boy

with fists. There was music in the background
and a clown walked by and looked and looked away.
She told you then, gold and practical advice.
You wanted one and craved the other.
Say "mother." No. *Say it.* No. *She shut the door?*
I wish she had. I saw the shadow cast there
on the floor. *What did you think?* I asked her,
actually. She said she hurt her lip. And
took a drink? Or the shadow did. I didn't think.
I knew she was lying. A child could see that.
You were a child. *Ah, this is the part*
where he parades his wound. He was a child.
It is the law of things: the little billy goat
goes first. Happily, he's not a morsel
for the troll. *Say "Dad, I've got a bite."*
That's different. Then you say, "Reel it in."
They're feeling fear and wonder, then.
That's when you teach them they can take the world
in hand. *You do?* Sometimes I do. Carefully.
They beat the child again when they get home.
All right. Assume the children are alright.
They're singing in the kibbutzim. The sun is rising.
Let's get past this part. The kindergarten
is a garden and they face their fears in stories
your voice makes musical and then they sleep.
They hear the sirens? *Yes, they hear the sirens.*
That part can't be helped. No one beats them, though.
And there are no lies they recognize. They know

you're with them and they fall asleep. What then?
Get past this part. It is a garden. Then they're grown.
What then? Say "groan." *I say what to say,*
you don't. They all ok, and grown. What then?

2.

Then? Then, the truth is, then they fall in love.
Oh no. *Oh yes.* Big subject. *Big shadow.*
I saw it slant across the floor, linoleum
in fact, and very dirty. Sad and dirty.
Because it lacked intention? Well, it did lack art.
Let's leave the shadow part alone. They fall in love.
What then? I want to leave this too.
It has its songs. Too many. I know them all.
It doesn't seem appropriate somehow. It was summer.
He saw her wandering through a field of grass.
It was the sweetest fire. Later, in the fall, it rained.
You loved her then? In rain? and gold October?
I would have died for her. *Tra-la.* Oh yes,
tra-la. We took long walks. You gather sadness
from a childhood to make a gift of it.
I gave her mine. *Some gift.* Is it so bad?
Sadness is a pretty word. Shadow's
shadow. And once there was a flood. Heavy rains,
and then the tide came in. I left her house
at midnight. It was pouring. I hitched a ride,

which stalled. The car in front of us had stopped.
The water rose across the road and ran downhill.
You'd forgotten this. I remember now. My knee
was in a cast. I hopped to the car in front,
the one that stalled. The driver's tongue stuck out,
a pale fat plum. His eyes bulged. An old man
in a gray felt hat. And the red lids flickered,
so he wasn't dead. *What did you do?* Got in,
shoved him aside, and tried to start the car.
What did you feel then? Wonderful. Like cleaning fish.
Your hands are bloody and you do the job.
It reminds you of a poem now? Yes,
the one about the fall that Bashō liked.
"The maple leaf becomes a midwife's hand."
The engine skipped and sank, twice. Then it started.
And I drove. The hospital was just a mile away
but near the creek. I thought the water
would be even higher. *Interesting, of course.*
This is the part about falling in love?
I left her house. We were necking, remember,
on a soft green velvet couch. *What then?*
I took the downhill road and floored it.
A gush spewed up and blurred the windshield.
I couldn't see a thing. The car sputtered,
surged, sputtered, surged, and died. And
he was dead. *Who was he?* Some old man.
That was the winter that you fell in love?
It was. *Did you feel bad?* No, I tried.

Do you believe in that? Now? I'm not sure.
He looked like a baby when they got him out
and raindrops bounced off raindrops on his face.
It didn't cost me anything.

      Anything?

4.

Privilege of Being

Many are making love. Up above, the angels
in the unshaken ether and crystal of human longing
are braiding one another's hair, which is strawberry blond
and the texture of cold rivers. They glance
down from time to time at the awkward ecstasy—
it must look to them like featherless birds
splashing in the spring puddle of a bed—
and then one woman, she is about to come,
peels back the man's shut eyelids and says,
look at me, and he does. Or is it the man
tugging the curtain rope in that dark theater?
Anyway, they do, they look at each other;
two beings with evolved eyes, rapacious,
startled, connected at the belly in an unbelievably sweet
lubricious glue, stare at each other,
and the angels are desolate. They hate it. They shudder pathetically
like lithographs of Victorian beggars
with perfect features and alabaster skin hawking rags
in the lewd alleys of the novel.
All of creation is offended by this distress.
It is like the keening sound the moon makes sometimes,
rising. The lovers especially cannot bear it,
it fills them with unspeakable sadness, so that
they close their eyes again and hold each other, each
feeling the mortal singularity of the body
they have enchanted out of death for an hour or so,
and one day, running at sunset, the woman says to the man,
I woke up feeling so sad this morning because I realized

that you could not, as much as I love you,
dear heart, cure my loneliness,
wherewith she touched his cheek to reassure him
that she did not mean to hurt him with this truth.
And the man is not hurt exactly,
he understands that life has limits, that people
die young, fail at love,
fail of their ambitions. He runs beside her, he thinks
of the sadness they have gasped and crooned their way out of
coming, clutching each other with old, invented
forms of grace and clumsy gratitude, ready
to be alone again, or dissatisfied, or merely
companionable like the couples on the summer beach
reading magazine articles about intimacy between the sexes
to themselves, and to each other,
and to the immense, illiterate, consoling angels.

Natural Theology

White daisies against the burnt orange of the windowframe,
lusterless redwood in the nickel gray of winter,
in the distance turbulence of water—the green regions
of the morning reflect whatever can be gained, normally,
by light, then give way to the blue regions of the afternoon
which do not reflect so much as they remember,
as if the light, one will all morning, yielded to a doubleness
in things—plucked skins of turkeys in an ill-lit butchershop
in the pitch-dark forenoon of a dreary day, or a stone bridge
in a small town, a cool café, tables with a violinback sheen,
ferns like private places of the body distanced and made cool—
images not quite left behind rising as an undertow
of endless transformation against the blurring world
outside the window where, after the morning clarities,
the faint reflection of a face appears; among the images
a road, repetitively, with meadow rue and yarrow
whitening its edges, and pines shadowing the cranberry brush,
and the fluting of one bird where the road curves and disappears,
becoming that gap or lack which is the oldest imagination
of need, defined more sharply by the silver-gray region
just before the sun goes down and the clouds fade
through rose to bruise to the city-pigeon color of a sky
going dark and the wind comes up in brushstroke silhouettes
of trees and to your surprise the window mirrors back to you
a face open, curious, and tender; as dance is defined
by the body's possibilities arranged, this dance

belongs to the composures and the running down of things
in the used sugars of five-thirty: a woman straightening
a desk turns her calendar to another day, signaling
that it is another day where the desk is concerned
and that there is in her days what doesn't belong to the desk;
a kid turns on TV, flops on the couch to the tinny sound
of little cartoon parents quarreling; a man in a bar
orders a drink, watches ice bob in the blond fluid,
he sighs and looks around; sad at the corners, nagged by wind,
others with packages; others dreaming, picking their noses
dreamily while they listen to the radio describe configurations
of the traffic they are stuck in as the last light
like held breath flickers among mudhens on the bay,
the black bodies elapsing as the dark comes on, and the face
in the window seems harder and more clear. The religion
or the region of the dark makes soup and lights a fire,
plays backgammon with children on the teeth or the stilettos
of the board, reads books, does dishes, listens
to the wind, listens to the stars imagined to be singing
invisibly, goes out to be regarded by the moon, walks
dogs, feeds cats, makes love in postures so various,
with such varying attention and intensity and hope,
it enacts the dispersion of tongues among the people
of the earth—*compris? versteh'*—and sleeps with sticky genitals
the erasures and the peace of sleep: exactly the half-moon
holds, and the city twinkles in particular windows, throbs

in its accumulated glow which is also and more blindingly
the imagination of need from which the sun keeps rising into
     morning light,
because desires do not split themselves up, there is one desire
touching the many things, and it is continuous.

Tahoe in August

What summer proposes is simply happiness:
heat early in the morning, jays
raucous in the pines. Frank and Ellen have a tennis game
at nine, Bill and Cheryl sleep on the deck
to watch a shower of summer stars. Nick and Sharon
stayed in, sat and talked the dark on,
drinking tea, and Jeanne walked into the meadow
in a white smock to write in her journal
by a grazing horse who seemed to want the company.
Some of them will swim in the afternoon.
Someone will drive to the hardware store to fetch
new latches for the kitchen door. Four o'clock;
the joggers jogging—it is one of them who sees
down the flowering slope the woman with her notebook
in her hand beside the white horse, gesturing, her hair
from a distance the copper color of the hummingbirds
the slant light catches on the slope; the hikers
switchback down the canyon from the waterfall;
the readers are reading, Anna is about to meet Vronsky,
that nice M. Swann is dining in Combray
with the aunts, and Carrie has come to Chicago.
What they want is happiness: someone to love them,
children, a summer by the lake. The woman who sets aside
her book blinks against the fuzzy dark,
re-entering the house. Her daughter drifts downstairs;
out late the night before, she has been napping,
and she's cross. Her mother tells her David telephoned.
"He's such a dear," the mother says, "I think

I make him nervous." The girl tosses her head as the horse
had done in the meadow while Jeanne read it her dream.
"You can call him now, if you want," the mother says,
"I've got to get the chicken started,
I won't listen." "Did I say you would?"
the girl says quickly. The mother who has been slapped
this way before and done the same herself another summer
on a different lake says, "Ouch." The girl shrugs
sulkily. "I'm sorry." Looking down: "Something
about the way you said that pissed me off."
"Hannibal has wandered off," the mother says,
wryness in her voice, she is thinking it is August,
"why don't you see if he's at the Finleys' house
again." The girl says, "God." The mother: "He loves
small children. It's livelier for him there."
The daughter, awake now, flounces out the door,
which slams. It is for all of them the sound of summer.
The mother she looks like stands at the counter snapping beans.

Thin Air

What if I did not mention death to get started
or how love fails in our well-meaning hands
or what my parents in the innocence of their malice
toward each other did to me. What if I let the light
pour down on the mountain meadow, mule ears
dry already in the August heat, and the sweet
heavy scent of sage rising into it, marrying
what light it can, a wartime marriage,
summer is brief in these mountains, the
ticker-tape parade of snow will bury it
in no time, in the excess the world gives
up there, and down here, you want snow? you think
you have seen infinity watching the sky shuffle
the pink cards of thirty thousand flamingoes
on the Sengereti Plain? this is my blush,
she said, turning toward you, eyes downcast
demurely, a small smile playing at her mouth,
playing what? house, playing I am the sister
and author of your sorrow, playing the Lord
God loves the green earth and I am a nun
of his Visitations, you want snow, I'll give you
snow, she said, this is my flamingoes-in-migration
blush. Winter will bury it. You had better
sleep through that cold, or sleep in a solitary bed
in a city where the stone glistens darkly
in the morning rain, you are allowed a comforter,
silky in texture though it must be blue,
and you can listen to music in the morning,

the notes nervous as light reflected in a fountain,
and you can drink your one cup of fragrant tea
and rinse the cup and sweep your room and
the sadness you are fighting off while the gulls'
calls beat about the church towers out the window
and you smell the salt smell of the sea
is the dream you don't remember of the meadow
sleeping under fifteen feet of snow though you half
recall the tracks of some midsized animal,
a small fox or a large hare, and the deadly
silence, and the blinded-eye gray of the winter sky:
it is sleeping, the meadow, don't wake it.
You have to go to the bottom of the raveling.
The surgical pan, and the pump, and the bits
of life that didn't take floating in the smell
of alcohol, or the old man in the bed spitting up
black blood like milk of the other world, or the way
middle-aged women from poorer countries are the ones
who clean up after and throw the underwear away.
Hang on to the luxury of the way she used
to turn to you, don't abandon it, summer
is short, no one ever told you differently,
this is a good parade, this is the small hotel,
the boathouse on the dock, and the moon thin,
just silvering above the pines, and you are starting
to sweat now, having turned north out of the meadow
and begun the ascent up granite and through buckthorn
to the falls. There is a fine film on your warm skin

that you notice. You are water, light and water and thin air,
and you're breathing deeply now—a little dead marmot
like a rag of auburn hair swarms with ants beside the trail—
and you can hear the rush of water in the distance
as it takes its leap into the air and falls. In the winter
city she is walking toward you or away from you,
the fog condensing and dripping from the parapets
of old apartments and from the memory of intimate garments
that dried on the balcony in summer, even in the spring.
Do you understand? You can brew your one cup of tea
and you can drink it, the leaves were grown in Ceylon,
the plump young man who packed them was impatient,
he is waiting for news of a scholarship to Utrecht,
he is pretty sure he will rot in this lousy place
if he doesn't get it, and you can savor the last sip,
rinse the cup, and put it on the shelf,
and then you go outside or you sit down at the desk.
You go into yourself, the sage scent rising in the heat.

Between the Wars

When I ran, it rained. Late in the afternoon—
midsummer, upstate New York, mornings I wrote,
read Polish history, and there was a woman
whom I thought about; outside the moody, humid
American sublime—late in the afternoon,
toward sundown, just as the sky was darkening,
the light came up and redwings settled in the cattails.
They were death's idea of twilight, the whole notes
of a requiem the massed clouds croaked
above the somber fields. *Lady of eyelashes,*
do you hear me? Whiteness, otter's body,
coolness of the morning, rubbed amber
and the skin's salt, do you hear me? This is Poland speaking,
"era of the dawn of freedom," nineteen twenty-two.
When I ran, it rained. The blackbirds settled
their clannish squabbles in the reeds, and light came up.
First darkening, then light. And then pure fire.
Where does it come from? out of the impure
shining that rises from the soaked odor of the grass,
the levitating, Congregational, meadow-light-at-twilight
light that darkens the heavy-headed blossoms
of wild carrot, out of that, out of nothing
it boils up, pools on the horizon, fissures up,
igniting the undersides of clouds: pink flame,
red flame, vermilion, purple, deeper purple, dark.
You could wring the sourness of the sumac from the air,
the fescue sweetness from the grass, the slightly
maniacal cicadas tuning up to tear the fabric

of the silence into tatters, so that night,
if it wants to, comes as a beggar to the door
at which, if you do not offer milk and barley
to the maimed figure of the god, your well will foul,
your crops will wither in the fields. In the eastern marches
children know the story that the aspen quivers
because it failed to hide the Virgin and the Child
when Herod's hunters were abroad. Think: night is the god
dressed as the beggar drinking the sweet milk.
Gray beard, thin shanks, the look in the eyes
idiot, unbearable, the wizened mouth agape,
like an infant's that has cried and sucked and cried
and paused to catch its breath. The pink nubbin
of the nipple glistens. I'll suckle at that breast,
the one in the song of the muttering illumination
of the fields before the sun goes down, before
the black train crosses the frontier from Prussia
into Poland in the age of the dawn of freedom.
Fifty freight cars from America, full of medicine
and the latest miracle, canned food.
The war is over. There are unburied bones
in the fields at sun-up, skylarks singing,
starved children begging chocolate on the tracks.

On Squaw Peak

I don't even know which sadness
it was came up
in me when we were walking down the road to Shirley Lake,
the sun gleaming in snowpatches,
the sky so blue it seemed the light's dove
of some pentecost of blue,
the mimulus, yellow, delicate of petal,
and the pale yellow cinquefoil trembling in the damp
air above the creek, —
and fields of lupine,
that blue blaze of lupine, a swath of paintbrush
sheening it, and so much of it, long meadows
of it gathered out of the mountain air and spilling
down ridge toward the lake it almost looked like
in the wind. I think I must have thought
the usual things: that the flowering season
in these high mountain meadows is so brief, that
the feeling, something like hilarity, of sudden
pleasure when you first come across some tough little plant
you knew you'd see comes because it seems—I mean
by *it* the larkspur or penstemon curling
and arching the reach of its sexual being
up out of a little crack in granite—to say
that human hunger has a niche up here in the light-cathedral
of the dazzled air. I wanted to tell you
that when the ghost-child died, the three-month dreamer
she and I would never know, I kept feeling that
the heaven it went to was like the inside of a store window

on a rainy day from which you watch the blurred forms
passing in the street. Or to tell you, more terrible,
that when she and I walked off the restlessness
of our misery afterward in the Coast Range hills,
we saw come out of the thicket shyly
a pure white doe. I wanted to tell you I knew
it was a freak of beauty like the law of averages
that killed our child and made us know, as you had said,
that things between lovers, even of longest standing,
can be botched in their bodies, though their wills don't fail.
Still later, on the beach, we watched the waves.
No two the same size. No two in the same arch
of rising up and pouring. But it is the same law.
You shell a pea, there are three plump seeds and one
that's shriveled. You shell a bushelful and you begin
to feel the rhythms of the waves at Limantour,
glittering, jagged, that last bright October afternoon.
It killed something in me, I thought, or froze it,
to have to see where beauty comes from. I imagined
for a long time that the baby, since
it would have liked to smell our clothes to know
what a mother and a father would have been,
hovered sometimes in our closet and I half expected
to see it there, half-fish spirit, form of tenderness,
a little dead dreamer with open eyes. That was
private sorrow. I tried not to hate my life,
to fear the frame of things. I knew what two people
couldn't say

on a cold November morning in the fog—
you remember the feel of Berkeley winter mornings—
what they couldn't say to each other
was the white deer not seen. It meant to me
that beauty and terror were intertwined so powerfully
and went so deep that any kind of love
can fail. I didn't say it. I think the mountain startled
my small grief. Maybe there wasn't time.
We may have been sprinting to catch the tram
because we had to teach poetry
in that valley two thousand feet below us.
You were running—Steven's mother, Michael's lover,
mother and lover, grieving, of a girl
about to leave for school and die to you a little
(or die into you, or simply turn away)—
and you ran like a gazelle,
in purple underpants, royal purple,
and I laughed out loud. It was the abundance
the world gives, the more-than-you-bargained-for
surprise of it, waves breaking,
the sudden fragrance of the mimulus at creekside
sharpened by the summer dust.
Things bloom up there. They are
for their season alive in those bright vanishings
of air we ran through.

ROBERT HASS is the author of four books of poems, *Field Guide* (1973), *Praise* (1979), *Human Wishes* (1989) and *Sun Under Wood* (1996). He is the recipient of the William Carlos Williams Award for *Praise*, and two National Book Critics Circle Awards, in criticism for *Twentieth Century Pleasures: Prose on Poetry*, and in poetry for *Sun Under Wood*. His many other honors include fellowships from the John D. and Catherine T. MacArthur Foundation and the Guggenheim Foundation, an award of merit from the American Academy of Arts and Letters, and the PEN award for translation. He served as Poet Laureate of the United States from 1995 to 1997. Robert Hass teaches at the University of California, Berkeley.

Notes

Page 11 *"Rusia en 1931"* is the original title of a book about the
Soviet Union published in Paris in 1931 by César Vallejo.
The archbishop is the Reverend Oscar Romero. Since this
poem was written, his assassination has been clearly
linked to El Salvador's right-wing death squads.

Page 42 "Santa Lucia II." Santa Lucia is the name of the virgin
saint to whom several early Christian legends are attached,
and also of a mountain range on the central California
coast. The speaker in this poem is a woman who,
apparently, writes about art professionally. The first part
of this poem can be found in my earlier volume *Praise*.

Page 60 "Berkeley Eclogue." The phrase "a century of clouds" is
borrowed, of course, from Guillaume Apollinaire, but also
from a book of stories with that title by Bruce Boone,
published by Black Star Press.